THE OFFICIAL
TOTTENHAM HOTSPUR
ANNUAL 2021

TOTTENHAM
HOTSPUR

Written by **Andy Greeves**

Designed by **Daniel May**

g

A Grange Publication

© 2020. Published by Grange Communications Ltd., Edinburgh, under licence from Tottenham Hotspur Ltd. Printed in the EU.

Photographs © Getty Images & PA Images

ISBN: 978-1-913578-06-0

CONTENTS

INTRODUCTION

Dear Supporters,

Welcome to the 2021 Official Tottenham Hotspur Annual.

The 2019/20 Premier League season saw us achieve qualification to a European competition for an 11th consecutive season as we finished sixth in the Premier League and reached the UEFA Europa League.

The campaign saw memorable victories over the likes of Arsenal, Manchester City and West Ham United while we progressed to the knockout phases of the UEFA Champions League. A comprehensive review of the 2019/20 season can be found in this Annual.

We also find out more about our Head Coach Jose Mourinho and his coaching staff, and profile our talented squad of players. Sixty years on from our 'Double' winning success in 1960/61, we reflect on our season of seasons under the management of the legendary Bill Nicholson. We also look to the future and Spurs' interest in the upcoming UEFA European Championships.

Elsewhere, we introduce our new signings and explore Tottenham Hotspur Stadium, while there are quizzes, games, posters and plenty more besides.

Enjoy your new Annual and COME ON YOU SPURS!

#COYS
Andy Greeves

PREMIER LEAGUE
SEASON REVIEW 2019/20

The 2019/20 season saw Spurs finish sixth in the Premier League and secure qualification to the UEFA Europa League for the following campaign. We won 16 of our 38 league matches during the season while we drew 11 and lost 11 fixtures as we scored 61 goals and conceded 47 in the process. For the sixth successive season, Harry Kane was our top scorer, with 18 Premier League goals and 24 strikes overall. In 2020/21, we will be playing European football for an 11th consecutive season by virtue of our finishing position in the Premier League. We haven't finished outside the division's top six since the 2008/09 campaign, when we came eighth.

AUGUST

Tanguy Ndombele scored on his competitive Spurs debut as we beat Aston Villa 3-1 in our opening match of the 2019/20 Premier League season. The Frenchman's 73rd-minute equaliser came after we had fallen behind to a first-half strike from John McGinn. Harry Kane bagged a late brace as we secured all three points.

The following week, a fine individual effort from Erik Lamela helped us to a 2-2 draw with Manchester City. Lucas Moura was also on target at the Etihad Stadium while Raheem Sterling and Sergio Agüero scored for the home side. The month ended with a disappointing 1-0 home defeat to Newcastle United.

A Christian Eriksen strike and a Kane penalty put us 2-0 up in the 186th north London derby at the start of September. Alexandre Lacazette got a goal back for Arsenal in stoppage time at the end of the first period and Pierre-Emerick Aubameyang levelled in the second half in an entertaining 2-2 draw at the Emirates Stadium.

After the international break, Heung-Min Son scored twice while a Patrick van Aanholt own-goal and a Lamela effort sealed a 4-0 win over Crystal Palace at Tottenham Hotspur Stadium.

Kane's fourth goal of the season wasn't enough to prevent us going down to a 2-1 defeat at Leicester City but we returned to winning ways seven days later with a 2-1 home triumph over Southampton. Ndombele and Kane were on target against the Saints.

SEPTEMBER

OCTOBER

Hugo Lloris suffered a serious injury in a 3-0 defeat at Brighton & Hove Albion in October that saw him ruled out of action for almost four months. A late Dele Alli goal helped us pick up a point as we drew 1-1 with Watford at Tottenham Hotspur Stadium a few weeks later, then we went down to a 2-1 defeat to eventual champions Liverpool at Anfield, despite Kane putting us in front in the first minute of the match.

NOVEMBER

Cenk Tosun scored in the seventh minute of stoppage time at the end of a 1-1 draw at Everton. We had taken a 67th minute lead in the game through Dele. Another late concession saw us draw 1-1 with Sheffield United at Tottenham Hotspur Stadium. Son got our opening goal that day.

Jose Mourinho's first match as Spurs head coach resulted in a 3-2 away win at West Ham United. We led 3-0 at the London Stadium through goals from Son, Lucas and Kane before the Hammers reduced their arrears with strikes from Michail Antonio and Angelo Ogbonna.

Our second successive 3-2 Premier League win saw us establish a three-goal lead once again, as we beat AFC Bournemouth in N17. A Dele brace and a rare Moussa Sissoko strike came before substitute Harry Wilson got two goals for the Cherries.

DECEMBER

A busy December saw us play six Premier League matches in just 24 days. On our visit to Old Trafford, Dele displayed magnificent technique to equalise after Marcus Rashford had given Manchester United an early lead. Alas, a second-half Rashford penalty saw us go down to a 2-1 defeat.

We bounced back with our biggest Premier League victory of the season as we thrashed Burnley 5-0 at Tottenham Hotspur Stadium. Kane scored two excellent goals in the match but, by his own admission, saw Son "steal the thunder" from our vice-captain in the win. The South Korean's 32nd minute strike saw him sprint with the ball from the edge of his own penalty area before eventually slotting it past goalkeeper Nick Pope. His effort was voted as our Goal of the Season (see pages 42-43). Lucas and Sissoko also scored on a memorable afternoon in N17.

The disappointment of a 1-0 away defeat at Southampton on New Year's Day was exacerbated by an injury to Kane, that saw him ruled out until after the Premier League 'Restart' (see June). Ten days later, we were beaten 1-0 at home by Liverpool.

A goalless draw at Watford was followed by a 2-1 home victory over Norwich City. Dele and Son struck either side of a Teemu Pukki penalty for the Canaries as we sealed our first win of 2020.

The month continued with an excellent 2-1 victory against Wolverhampton Wanderers. Lucas gave us an eighth-minute lead at Molineux prior to Adama Traore's second-half leveller, but a stoppage time header from Jan Vertonghen secured us all three points.

After a 2-0 home defeat to Chelsea, we returned to Tottenham Hotspur Stadium for a Boxing Day clash with Brighton & Hove Albion. We trailed at half-time to Adam Webster's goal for the Seagulls but our players produced a

spirited second-half performance to win 2-1 thanks to strikes from Kane and Dele. The calendar year ended with a 2-2 draw at Norwich City a few days later. Eriksen and Kane (penalty) were on target at Carrow Road.

FEBRUARY

One of our most memorable wins of the season came at the start of February as we beat reigning champions Manchester City 2-0 at Tottenham Hotspur Stadium.

New signing Steven Bergwijn marked his Spurs debut with a superb effort from the edge of the City penalty area. Hugo Lloris saved a penalty from İlkay Gündoğan during the match while Son's 71st-minute goal confirmed our victory.

A brace from Son and a strike from Toby Alderweireld gave us a 3-2 win at Aston Villa before we went down to a 2-1 defeat to Chelsea at Stamford Bridge. An own-goal from Antonio Rudiger proved to be nothing more than a consolation for us that afternoon.

MARCH

Wolves got revenge for our 2-1 victory at Molineux earlier in the season as they won 3-2 at Tottenham Hotspur Stadium. Goals from Bergwijn and Serge Aurier, either side of Matt Doherty's 27th-minute effort for the visitors, saw us lead at half-time. Strikes from Diogo Jota and Raul Jimenez completed Wolves' comeback. The following weekend, Dele's penalty helped us to a 1-1 draw at Burnley.

On 13 March– two days before our scheduled home clash with Manchester United - the Premier League was suspended due to the COVID-19 pandemic.

The Premier League's 'Project Restart' saw the 2019/20 season resume on June 17 as Aston Villa drew 0-0 with Sheffield United. Owing to the health risks posed by COVID-19, no supporters were admitted to Premier League stadia for the remainder of the campaign. Our first 'behind-closed-doors' match following the restart took place on June 19, as we drew 1-1 with Manchester United at Tottenham Hotspur Stadium. Bergwijn got our goal against the Red Devils.

Kane's first goal of 2020 came in our 2-0 home victory over West Ham United four days later in a match in which the Hammers' Tomas Soucek also put through his own net.

Kane was on target again in our 3-1 defeat at Sheffield United while an own goal from Michael Keane brought us a 1-0 victory over Everton at Tottenham Hotspur Stadium.

Following a goalless draw at Bournemouth, goals from Son and Alderweireld helped us to a 2-1 win over Arsenal during a season in which we finished above our local rivals for a fourth consecutive campaign.

Kane continued his impressive goal-scoring run following the restart with a brace in a 3-1 win at Newcastle United, where Son was also on target. The England skipper also netted twice as we beat Leicester City 3-0 in N17, while the Foxes' James Justin scored an own goal.

A fifth goal in three Premier League matches for Kane helped us to a 1-1 draw at Crystal Palace on the final day of the campaign. The result, coupled with Wolves' 2-0 defeat at Chelsea, saw us finish sixth in the Premier League table and secure qualification for the UEFA Europa League.

EURO NIGHTS

Our fourth consecutive season in the UEFA Champions League in 2019/20 saw us progress to the last 16 of the competition.

GROUP G

MATCHDAY ONE
OLYMPIACOS 2-2 SPURS

Having been tripped in the penalty area by Olympiacos defender Yassine Meriah, Harry Kane picked himself up and scored from the resulting spot-kick in our opening Group B match of the 2019/20 season. Lucas Moura doubled our advantage on the half-hour mark with a powerful, right-footed shot from the edge of the 18-yard-box. Daniel Podence got a goal back for the home side just before half-time, while Mathieu Valbuena's 54th-minute penalty secured a point for the Greek side.

MATCHDAY TWO
SPURS 2-7 BAYERN MUNICH

We set an unwanted record in our heavy defeat to Bayern Munich, as we conceded seven goals in a home match for the first time in our history. Heung-Min Son put us one up just after 12 minutes of the game but strikes from Joshua Kimmich and Robert Lewandowski ensured Bayern held a 2-1 half-time lead. Serge Gnabry got four goals after the break while Kane's 61st-minute penalty proved little more than a consolation. Lewandowski got his second of the night shortly before the full-time whistle sounded to complete the scoring.

MATCHDAY THREE
SPURS 5-0 CRVENA ZVEZDA

Our players bounced back from the loss to Bayern with an emphatic display against Serbian side Crvena zvezda. A header from Kane and a brace from Son saw us command a three-goal, half-time lead. Erik Lamela – who had a hand in two of those three first-half goals – got on the scoresheet himself after the break, with a neat turn and shot past Milan Borjan. Kane made it five with an assured, right-footed finish.

MATCHDAY FOUR
CRVENA ZVEZDA 0-4 SPURS

Giovani Lo Celso scored his first Spurs goal in another comprehensive victory over Crvena zvezda. The Argentine converted on 34 minutes, following a goalmouth scramble that saw both Kane and Son hit the woodwork, while the South Korean international also had an effort cleared off the line. A neat team move involving Tanguy Ndombele and Dele Alli was finished by Son on 57 minutes while the same player netted again less than four minutes later. Christian Eriksen rounded off the scoring to put us within touching distance of the last 16.

MATCHDAY FIVE
SPURS 4-2 OLYMPIACOS

Progression to the knockout phase of the Champions League was completed with our third consecutive Group B win. We had to come from behind to secure victory in Jose Mourinho's first home match as Spurs manager, having conceded goals from Olympiacos' Youssef El-Arabi and Ruben Semedo in the opening 19 minutes of the game. Dele struck just before half-time and Kane equalised five minutes after the break before a curling half-volley from Serge Aurier put us in front. Kane's second strike of the night, with 13 minutes of normal time remaining, made sure of the win.

TO DARE IS TOTTENHAM

Introducing the new 2020/21 Tottenham Hotspur Home Kit

SHOP SPURS

MATCHDAY SIX
BAYERN MUNICH 3-1 SPURS

Ryan Sessegnon marked his first Spurs start with a fine first-half strike that drew us level in our Allianz Arena clash with Bayern Munich following Kingsley Coman's opener. Thomas Müller restored the home side's lead on the stroke of half-time while Philippe Coutinho's second-half goal confirmed victory for the Group B winners.

Group B Table	P	W	D	L	GF	GA	GD	PTS
Bayern Munich	6	6	0	0	24	5	+19	18
Spurs	6	3	1	2	18	14	+4	10
Olympiacos	6	1	1	4	8	14	-6	4
Crvena zvezda	6	1	0	5	3	20	-17	3

KNOCKOUT PHASE

ROUND OF 16, FIRST LEG
SPURS 0-1 RB LEIPZIG

A second-half penalty from Timo Werner put RB Leipzig 1-0 up after the first leg of our round of 16 tie with the German outfit. On a night in which Hugo Lloris made a string of fine saves, Lo Celso came close to scoring for us as his free-kick was forced on to the post by Leipzig keeper Peter Gulacsi.

ROUND OF 16, SECOND LEG
RB LEIPZIG 3-0 SPURS
(RB Leipzig win 4-0 on aggregate)

Our European adventures of 2019/20 came to an end at the Red Bull Arena as RB Leipzig wrapped up a 4-0 aggregate victory in our round of 16 tie. A brace from Marcel Sabitzer put the home side two-up within the opening 21 minutes of the match while a late strike from Emil Forsberg confirmed a 3-0 win on the night for the Bundesliga outfit.

THIRD ROUND
MIDDLESBROUGH 1-1 SPURS

We faced our former players Jonathan Woodgate and Robbie Keane – manager and assistant manager respectively of Middlesbrough – as we travelled to the Riverside Stadium for an FA Cup third round tie. Ashley Fletcher gave the hosts the lead five minutes after half-time but we levelled just after the hour mark as Lucas Moura headed in from a Serge Aurier cross.

THIRD ROUND REPLAY
SPURS 2-1 MIDDLESBROUGH

Goals from Argentines Giovani Lo Celso and Erik Lamela put us two-up in the opening 15 minutes of our third round replay with Middlesbrough. A late strike from George Saville proved to be nothing more than a consolation for the EFL Championship side.

FA CUP 2019/20

FOURTH ROUND
SOUTHAMPTON 1-1 SPURS

A second-half goal from Heung-Min Son gave us the lead in our fourth round clash with fellow Premier League side Southampton. A late equaliser from Sofiane Boufal set up a replay at the Tottenham Hotspur Stadium.

FOURTH ROUND REPLAY
SPURS 3-2 SOUTHAMPTON

A deflected shot from Tanguy Ndombele - which hit Southampton defender Jack Stephens before hitting the back of the net – put us in front in an entertaining FA Cup fourth round replay. Shane Long levelled for Saints on 34 minutes after Nathan Redmond's shot was parried by Hugo Lloris. Danny Ings put the visitors 2-1 up with 18 minutes of normal time remaining before a goal from Lucas and a penalty from Son restored our lead and saw us through to round five.

FIFTH ROUND
SPURS 1-1 NORWICH CITY
(Norwich win 3-2 on penalties)

With no replays in the FA Cup beyond the fourth round stage, our fifth round match with Norwich City ended up being settled with a penalty shootout. Jan Vertonghen put us in front after 13 minutes of the tie, heading in from a Lo Celso cross. Josip Drmić's close-range effort with 12 minutes of the match remaining forced extra time and with no further goals in the added period. The Canaries ended up winning 3-2 on spot-kicks.

CARABAO CUP 2019/20

THIRD ROUND
COLCHESTER UNITED 0-0 SPURS
(Colchester win 4-3 on penalties)

Having reached the semi-final of the competition the previous season, we were eliminated from the Carabao Cup at the third round stage in 2019/20. Despite having 75% possession and 19 shots, we were unable to break down Colchester's stubborn defence during a goalless 90 minutes at the JobServe Community Stadium. Our first effort of the ensuing penalty shootout saw U's goalkeeper Dean Gerken save from Christian Eriksen prior to successful conversions from Dele Alli, Erik Lamela and Heung-Min Son. Paulo Gazzaniga kept out Jevani Brown's 'Panenka' spot-kick to level the score at one stage but Lucas Moura smashed our fifth effort against the woodwork as the home side triumphed 4-3 on penalties.

YOUTH TEAMS
ROUND-UP 2019/20

Our youth teams saw their various 2019/20 league competitions cancelled in May 2020 prior to their conclusion, as a result of the COVID-19 pandemic.

Premier League 2

The 2019/20 Premier League 2 season was suspended and eventually curtailed due to the COVID-19 pandemic. The sporting outcoming of the division was determined by Points Per Game. We finished 10th in the table having won six, drawn three and lost nine of our 17 matches in the division.

Under-18 Premier League South

Our last match prior to the cancellation of the 2019/20 Under-18 Premier League South was an impressive 6-1 win over Southampton at the end of February. As per the Premier League 2, Points Per Game was also used to finalise positions in the Under-18 division. We ended up fifth in the table, having won eight, drawn two and lost seven of our 17 matches.

UEFA Youth League

Kion Etete

The highlight of our 2019/20 UEFA Youth League campaign was a comprehensive 9-2 victory over Crvena zvezda at Hotspur Way in October 2019. Troy Parrott scored four goals in the win, including a 75th-minute penalty. In our other Group B fixtures, we drew 1-1 in our away match at Olympiacos and beat the Greek side 1-0 at home, while we lost our away game at Crvena Zvezda and both fixtures with Bayern Munich.

EFL Trophy

Our Under-21 side faced senior opposition in their three EFL Trophy Group A (Southern Section) fixtures in 2019/20. We went down to a

vs Olympiacos

2-1 defeat to Ipswich Town in the first of those matches. A strike from Tashan Oakley-Boothe saw us take Colchester United to a penalty shoot-out following a 1-1 draw at the Colchester Community Stadium. We triumphed 6-5 on spot-kicks. A 2-0 defeat to Gillingham in our final group fixture saw us eliminated from the competition.

Under-18 Premier League Cup

We bounced back from a 2-1 defeat to West Ham United in our opening 2019/20 Under-18 Premier League Cup fixture to beat Stoke City 3-2 at Hotspur Way. A 5-2 defeat at Newcastle United in November prevented our progress to the next round of the competition.

FA Youth Cup

We overcame FA Youth Cup holders Liverpool with an impressive 4-2 victory at Stevenage's Lamex Stadium in December 2019. A brace from Troy Parrott and further goals from Max Robson and Chay Cooper saw us through to the fourth round, where we suffered a 2-0 away defeat to Wigan Athletic.

Chay Cooper

TOTTENHAM HOTSPUR WOMEN 2019/20

Owing to the outbreak of the COVID-19 pandemic, the Barclays FA Women's Super League (WSL) 2019/20 season was cancelled in May 2020 prior to the completion of the campaign. In our historic first season in the top flight of women's league football, Karen Hills and Juan Amoros' team were eventually awarded a seventh-place finish in the WSL table after 15 rounds of fixtures, while we progressed to the quarter-finals of the Women's FA Cup.

Lucy Quinn

SEPTEMBER

A crowd of 24,564 watched our inaugural WSL fixture, as we went down to a 1-0 defeat to Chelsea at Stamford Bridge on 8 September 2019. We didn't have to wait long for our first victory in the division, which arrived a week later on our home debut at The Hive. Rachel Furness' first-half penalty was enough to give us a 1-0 home triumph over Liverpool.

Another bumper crowd of 24,790 were present at the London Stadium as we beat West Ham United 2-0. Rianna Dean scored the opener in the first half, while Lucy Quinn doubled our advantage with just six minutes of the 90 remaining.

OCTOBER

After a 3-0 defeat to Manchester United at The Hive, we returned to winning ways with a 2-1 triumph away at Bristol City. Kit Graham scored two long-range stunners with her left foot in the space of two second-half minutes to guarantee us the three points.

Kit Graham

NOVEMBER

A WSL record attendance of 38,262 saw our north London derby against local rivals Arsenal at Tottenham Hotspur Stadium on 17 November 2019. Despite a spirited showing from the team, it was the Gunners who triumphed 2-0 that afternoon. The month also saw a 3-1 defeat at Everton.

DECEMBER

A second-half equaliser from Graham helped us to a 1-1 draw at Birmingham City, while an own goal from Victoria Williams gave us a 1-0 win over Brighton & Hove Albion at The Hive at the start of December. Despite a 6-0 home win over Lewes - which included an Angela Addison hat-trick and a Quinn brace – we exited the FA Women's Continental League Cup, having finished fourth in our six-team group. Chelsea

Rianna Dean

and Reading progressed to the knockout phase from Group D. The year ended with a 3-1 WSL away defeat to Reading.

JANUARY

Sandwiched in between defeats to Manchester City and Manchester United, goals from Emma Mitchell and Dean gave us a 2-1 home victory over West Ham United in the WSL. Dean also got two goals in our 5-0 thrashing of National League Division One side Barnsley, as our Women's FA Cup adventure got underway. Siri Worm and Gemma Davison also netted in the fourth round victory.

Siri Worm

FEBRUARY

Our last WSL fixtures prior to the suspension and subsequent cancellation of the league saw us draw 2-2 at home to Everton and win 1-0 at Brighton & Hove Albion. Addison and Mitchell were on target in our match-up with the Toffees, while Dean got our winner against the Seagulls. Our Women's FA Cup progress continued with a 5-0 away win at Coventry City. A hat-trick from Dean and further goals from Worm and Lucia Leon set-up a quarter-final tie with rivals Arsenal prior to the suspension of the competition. The resolution of the 2019/20 Women's FA Cup was still under review at the time of writing this Annual.

When the 2019/20 WSL Season was suspended, we were sixth in the league table, having won six, drawn two and lost seven of our 15 matches. Upon the cancellation of the remaining league fixtures, we were awarded a seventh-place finish in the division, with the final standings decided on a 'points per game' (PPG) basis.

JOSE MOURINHO

Jose Mourinho became our Head Coach in November 2019, putting pen to paper on a contract that runs until the end of the 2022/23 season.

Born in Setubal, Portugal on 26 January 1963, the former midfielder represented the likes of Rio Ave, Belenenses, Sesimbra and Comercio e Industria during his playing career. After hanging up his boots in 1987, his early coaching roles saw him work at Vitoria de Setubal and Estrela da Amadora. He was also a scout for Ovarense.

In 1992, Jose took a job as a translator for the legendary Sir Bobby Robson at Sporting CP. He followed Robson to work as his assistant manager at Porto in 1993 and Barcelona in 1996, while he also served as Louis van Gaal's right-hand man at Barcelona. His first managerial post came at Benfica in 2000 while he took the top job at Uniao de Leiria a year later.

Jose shone as manager of Porto between 2002 and 2004, where he won two Primeira Liga titles, the UEFA Cup in 2003 and the UEFA Champions League a year later. He followed that up with an impressive three-year stint at Chelsea, where he collected two Premier League titles, two Football League Cups and the FA Cup.

Success continued at Inter Milan, who he guided to back-to-back Scudetti in 2009 and 2010, as well as the Coppa Italia and the UEFA Champions League in 2010. He was a La Liga winner with Real Madrid in 2012, where he had also won the Copa del Ray a year earlier. Jose's return to English football and to Chelsea in 2013 saw the Blues go on to win the Premier League and

Football League Cup in 2015. He then lifted the Football League Cup and UEFA Europa League with Manchester United in 2017.

Jose has won 25 major senior trophies to date and is the only manager to have won a top-flight league title in four different European countries (Portugal, England, Italy and Spain). He is a three-time Premier League Manager of the Season and a four-time winner of the IFFHS World's Best Club Coach award. He was also named UEFA Manager of the Year in both 2003 and 2004 as well as the FIFA World Coach of the Year in 2010.

Jose's first match as our Head Coach saw us win 3-2 at West Ham United on 23 November 2019. In his inaugural season in charge, he guided us to a sixth-place finish in the Premier League, the UEFA Champions League round of 16 and the FA Cup fifth round.

JOSE'S SPURS RECORD

Played: **35**   Drawn: **9**

Won: **16**   Lost: **10**

Win percentage: **45.71%**

MEET JOSE'S COACHING STAFF

JOAO SACRAMENTO
Assistant Head Coach

Joao Sacramento joined us as Assistant Head Coach in November, 2019.

Born in Barcelos, Portugal on 31 January, 1989, Joao was a youth academy player with SC Braga prior to moving to the United Kingdom. He has a BSc in Sports Coaching and Development and a MSc in Advanced Performance Football Coaching from the University of South Wales, having obtained the latter qualification in 2012. He also served as a video analyst for the Welsh national team during his studies.

In February, 2014, he joined Ligue 1 club AS Monaco as Head of Tactical Analysis, serving under the stewardship of both Claudio Ranieri and Leonardo Jardim before being appointed as Assistant Coach at LOSC Lille in January, 2017.

LEDLEY KING
First-Team Assistant

As a Spurs legend who made 323 competitive appearances and scored 14 goals for us between 1999 and 2012, Ledley King needs little introduction. A one-club man during his playing career, Ledley served as an Ambassador for us after hanging up his boots in 2012. In the summer of 2020, we announced that the former England international defender would be joining as a member of our first team staff, working alongside the coaches, analysts and playing squad both at the Training Centre and on matchdays. He will also take on the role of supporting our academy players as they look to step up to the first team.

NUNO SANTOS
Goalkeeper Coach

Former goalkeeper Nuno Santos represented the likes of Vitoria Setubal, Benfica, Santa Clara and Toronto FC – and was also on the books at Leeds United between 1998 and 1999 – prior to retiring from playing in 2012 at the age of 39.

Following the conclusion of his playing career, Nuno attained UEFA Pro and UEFA A Licence coaching badges and worked as Goalkeeper Coach of the Canadian national team and served as a Goalkeeper Coach at LOSC Lille between 2018 and 2019 prior to joining us.

CARLOS LALIN
Head of First Team Performance

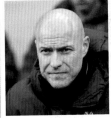

Born in Caracas, Venezuela on 4 August, 1970, Carlos Lalin spent 10 years on the coaching staff at Deportivo La Coruña before moving to Real Madrid for a further six years, where he first worked under Jose Mourinho. He subsequently linked up the Portuguese Head Coach at Chelsea, Manchester United and now at Spurs.

GIOVANNI CERRA
Technological Analyst

Giovanni Cerra helps to evaluate and improve team performance by analysing match data and statistics. Through the use of technology such as coding and 'telestration', he produces infographics and video reports to offer the players gain a better understanding of the game.

PLAYER PROFILES

Due to the extension of the summer transfer window, we had to print this edition before the window closed. There may, therefore, be some players listed over these pages who have since departed the Club while new signings made after we went to print will not feature.

HUGO **LLORIS**

The 2020/21 season is Club captain Hugo Lloris' ninth campaign with us, having joined from Olympique Lyonnais back in 2012. The Frenchman, who made his 300th appearance in our colours in the 2-2 draw at Manchester City in August 2019, holds the Club record for the most Premier League clean sheets, with 92 stop-outs in the division as of the end of the 2019/20 season. Hugo has played over 100 times for France and lifted the World Cup in 2018 as skipper of Les Bleus.

PAULO **GAZZANIGA**

With Hugo Lloris sidelined by an injury for several months during the 2019/20 season, Paulo Gazzaniga made 25 appearances for us during the campaign, including four starts in the UEFA Champions League. The Argentine, who joined us from Southampton in August 2017, made his Spurs debut in a 1-0 win over Crystal Palace in November that year. He impressed with two penalty saves during our 4-2 shootout victory over Watford after a 2-2 draw in a Carabao Cup third round tie in September 2018. He made his international debut for Argentina in their 2-0 win against Mexico a few months later.

JOE **HART**

Joe Hart joined us in the summer of 2020 having left Burnley at the end of the 2019/20 campaign. The experienced goalkeeper began his career with his home town club, Shrewsbury Town, prior to a transfer to Manchester City in 2006. He won two Premier League titles, two League Cups and an FA Cup during a 12-year spell at the Etihad Stadium, during which time he collected four Premier League Golden Glove awards and was twice named in the PFA Team of the Year. The England international, who has 75 caps to his name at the time of writing, was loaned to Torino and West Ham United during his time as a City player.

DANNY **ROSE**

Danny Rose joined us from Leeds United back in July 2007 and has since featured in over 200 competitive matches for us. He made 16 appearances for us in the first half of the 2019/20 season before spending the remainder of the campaign on loan at Newcastle United. The versatile player, who operates predominantly at left-back, played for England at all levels between U16 and U21 before making his senior Three Lions debut against Germany in March 2016.

TOBY **ALDERWEIRELD**

Toby Alderweireld put pen to paper on a new contract with us in December 2019 that will keep him at the Club until 2023. The Belgium international joined us from Atletico Madrid in July 2015. He made his Spurs debut against Manchester United in August 2015, while his 200th Club appearance came in our 3-0 victory over Leicester City in July 2020. He netted twice in 42 matches during the 2019/20 season in wins over Aston Villa and Arsenal.

DAVINSON **SANCHEZ**

Colombian international Davinson Sanchez joined us from Ajax in August 2017 for a Club record fee. The defender has since played in over 100 matches for us, including eight appearances during our memorable UEFA Champions League campaign of 2018/19 that saw us reach the final. He put pen-to-paper on an improved contact after his debut season with the Club in 2017/18, committing his future with us until 2024.

SERGE **AURIER**

Right back Serge Aurier joined us from Paris Saint-Germain in August 2017. The Ivory Coast international netted twice in 24 appearances in his inaugural campaign in our colours in 2017/18 and followed that up with two strikes in 17 matches for us in 2018/19. He scored twice in 42 fixtures in 2019/20, which included a memorable volley against Olympiacos in the UEFA Champions League.

BEN **DAVIES**

A consistent and reliable performer, Ben Davies was closing in on his 200th Spurs appearance at the time of writing this Annual. Born in Neath on 24 April 1993, the Welshman rose through the ranks at Swansea City to establish himself as a First Team player, making 85 senior appearances between 2012 and 2014. The defender signed for Spurs in July 2014 and put pen to paper on a new, five-year contract with us in July 2019.

JUAN **FOYTH**

Defender Juan Foyth arrived from Estudiantes in the summer of 2017 and made 23 appearances in his first two seasons at Spurs. Subsequently he played in seven matches for us in 2019/20. His first goal came in our 1-0 win at Crystal Palace in the Premier League in November 2018, while he also made his senior debut for Argentina against Mexico in a 2-0 victory that same month.

ERIC **DIER**

Eric Dier signed a new contract with us in July 2020, extending his stay through until 2024. The versatile player, who is able to operate in defence or midfield, originally joined us from Sporting Lisbon in August 2014 and scored the winning goal at West Ham United on his Spurs debut that month. He has since featured in over 200 matches for us and has been a regular member of the England senior squad.

PIERRE-EMILE **HØJBJERG**

Pierre-Emile Højbjerg joined us in August 2020 after four seasons with Southampton, where he scored five goals in 134 appearances. The dynamic midfielder started his professional career with Bundesliga giants Bayern Munich, for whom he became the club's youngest league debutant in April 2013, at the age of 17 years and 251 days. More information on the Danish international – who has also enjoyed loan spells with FC Augsburg and FC Schalke 04 during his career – can be found on pages 32 and 33 of this annual.

JAPHET **TANGANGA**

The 2019/20 season saw Spurs Academy graduate Japhet Tanganga establish himself as a member of our First Team squad. The defender made his competitive debut in a Carabao Cup tie at Colchester United in September 2019, while his first Premier League appearance came against Liverpool in January 2020. Following a campaign in which he featured in 11 matches in total, Japhet signed a new, five-year contract with us in July 2020.

MOUSSA **SISSOKO**

A French international with over 60 caps to his name, Moussa Sissoko has been an important member of our squad since joining from Newcastle United in 2016. He made 35 appearances for us across all competitions in 2019/20, scoring his first goal in over two years in our 3-2 Premier League victory over AFC Bournemouth in November 2019. He quickly followed that up with his second strike of the season in our 5-0 triumph over Burnley the following month. He made his 150th appearance for us against Brighton & Hove Albion on Boxing Day, 2019.

ERIK **LAMELA**

Erik Lamela marked his 200th Spurs appearance with an excellent performance in our 5-0 UEFA Champions League victory over Crvena Zvezda in October 2019. The Argentine international scored and made two assists on the night, and netted four times in 35 appearances in total in 2019/20. Erik joined us from Roma in 2013 and is well-known for the 'rabona' goal he scored against Asteras Tripoli in October 2014 which was subsequently named the UEFA Europa League 'Goal of the Season'. He had scored three times in 25 matches for Argentina at of the end of 2019/20 season.

DELE **ALLI**

Dele Alli's fifth season at Spurs in 2019/20 saw him score nine times in 38 matches in all competitions. The attacking midfielder joined the likes of Toby Alderweireld, Erik Lamela and Heung-Min Son in making his 200th appearance for us during the campaign, achieving the landmark as he started in our 2-1 win at Wolverhampton Wanderers in December 2019. Born in Milton Keynes on 11 April 1996, Dele started his career with his local professional side MK Dons before signing for us in 2015. The two-time PFA Young Player of the Year (2016 and 2017) has regularly featured in the England senior squad since making his Three Lions debut back in October 2015.

LUCAS MOURA

Lucas Moura will forever be remembered for his hat-trick in our 3-2 UEFA Champions League semi-final, second leg victory over Ajax in May 2019, which took us to the final of the competition. The Brazilian international also holds the distinction of being the first hat-trick scorer at Tottenham Hotspur Stadium by virtue of his trio in a 4-0 win over Huddersfield Town in April 2019. The former Sao Paulo and Paris Saint-Germain winger made his 100th Spurs appearance against West Ham United in June 2020.

HARRY WINKS

A lifelong Spurs fan, Harry Winks started training with us from the age of five prior to making his First Team debut in our 1-0 victory over FK Partizan in the UEFA Europa League in November 2014. He was a regular in the centre of our midfield during the 2019/20 season, featuring in 41 matches in all competitions. He scored his first senior goal for England on the occasion of his sixth international appearance in a 4-0 victory in Kosovo in November 2019.

TANGUY NDOMBELE

A new arrival prior to the start of the 2019/20 season, Tanguy Ndombele scored on his competitive debut for us in a 3-1 victory over Aston Villa in August, 2019. The Frenchman signed from Olympique Lyonnais and netted twice in 29 appearances in his inaugural season with us. The midfielder, who is a product EA Guingamp's youth system, made his senior international debut for France against Iceland in October 2018.

GIOVANI LO CELSO

Having impressed on loan from Spanish club Real Betis Balompie during the 2019/20 season, Giovani Lo Celso's contract was made permanent in January 2020 as he signed a contract running through to the summer of 2025. The attacking midfielder, who began his career with Rosario Central, signed for Paris Saint-Germain in 2016. The Argentinian international was initially loaned back to Rosario before scoring six goals in 54 appearances for PSG between 2016 and 2018. He moved to Real Betis - initially on loan, then permanently - during the 2018/19 season.

RYAN **SESSEGNON**

The highlight of Ryan Sessegnon's debut season with us in 2019/20 was a fine strike against Bayern Munich in the UEFA Champions League on his first Spurs start in December 2019. Ryan joined us from Fulham in the summer of 2019, having netted 25 times in 120 appearances for the Whites between 2016 and 2019. The Roehampton-born player, who has been capped for England at various levels between U16 and U21, was also an ever-present for Fulham in 2017/18 in the EFL Championship as they were promoted to the Premier League.

JACK **CLARKE**

York-born winger Jack Clarke signed a four-year contract with us in July 2019 prior to being loaned back to his original club, Leeds United. Clarke was also loaned to Queens Park Rangers during the second part of the 2019/20 season, for whom he featured in seven competitive matches. The player made his England U20 debut against Netherlands U20s in September 2019.

STEVEN **BERGWIJN**

Steven Bergwijn made quite an impact at Spurs following his arrival from PSV Eindhoven in January 2020, as he scored on his debut in a 2-0 Premier League victory over Manchester City. He went on to score further goals against Wolverhampton Wanderers and Manchester United during the campaign, which saw him make 16 appearances for us in total. The Dutchman has been capped at all levels between U17 and U21, while his senior Netherlands debut came against Germany in October 2018.

GEDSON **FERNANDES**

Gedson Fernandes joined us on an 18-month loan from Benfica in January 2020, making his Spurs debut in our goalless draw at Watford that month. The Portuguese winger made a total of 12 appearances for us during the 2019/20 season. Previously capped at U17, U19, U20 and U21 level, the player - who was born on the Central African island of Sao Tome and Principe – made his senior Portugal debut against Croatia in September 2018.

HEUNG-MIN **SON**

Heung-Min Son's impressive Spurs career continued in 2019/20 as he was named One Hotspur Player of the Season, One Hotspur Juniors' Player of the Season and Official Supporters' Clubs' Player of the Season for a second successive campaign (see pages 42-43). His individual goal against Burnley in December 2019 won our Goal of the Season award and was also voted the BBC Match of the Day's 'Goal of the Season' during a campaign in which he netted 18 times in 41 matches in all competitions. The South Korean international, who joined us from Bayer Leverkusen in 2015, made his 200th Spurs appearance against Liverpool in October 2019.

HARRY **KANE**

England captain Harry Kane netted 24 times in 34 appearances for us during the 2019/20 season as he moved up to third position on our top, all-time goal scorers list. The former Leyton Orient, Millwall, Norwich City and Leicester City loanee bagged his 200th and 201st club goals in our 3-1 away win against Newcastle United in July 2020, while he ended the 2019/20 campaign having scored 188 times in 287 Spurs appearances. The legendary Jimmy Greaves leads our scoring charts with 266 goals in 379 matches for the Club.

COYS

ROLL CALL
2019/20 SEASON

KEY:
FA – Full Appearances (i.e. In Starting line-up) • **SA** – Substitute Appearances (i.e. Used substitute) • **G** – Goals scored

PLAYER	PREMIER LEAGUE			FA CUP			EFL CUP			UEFA CHAMPIONS LEAGUE			TOTAL		
	FA	SA	G	FA	SA	G	FA	SA	G	FA	SA	G	FA	SA	G
Toby **Alderweireld**	33	0	2	3	0	0	0	0	0	6	0	0	42	0	2
Dele **Alli**	21	4	8	3	2	0	1	0	0	7	0	1	32	6	9
Serge **Aurier**	31	2	1	4	0	0	0	0	0	5	0	1	40	2	2
Steven **Bergwijn**	8	6	3	1	0	0	0	0	0	1	0	0	10	6	3
Ben **Davies**	16	2	0	0	0	0	1	0	0	3	0	0	20	2	0
Eric **Dier**	15	4	0	4	1	0	1	0	0	4	1	0	24	6	0
Christian **Eriksen**	10	10	2	2	0	0	0	1	0	2	3	1	14	14	3
Gedson **Fernandes**	0	7	0	1	2	0	0	0	0	1	1	0	2	10	0
Juan **Foyth**	1	3	0	0	0	0	0	0	0	2	1	0	3	4	0
Paulo **Gazzaniga**	17	1	0	2	0	0	1	0	0	4	0	0	24	1	0
Harry **Kane**	29	0	18	0	0	0	0	0	0	5	0	6	34	0	24
Erik **Lamela**	12	13	2	1	3	1	0	1	0	2	3	1	15	20	4
Hugo **Lloris**	22	0	0	2	0	0	0	0	0	4	0	0	27	0	0
Giovani **Lo Celso**	15	13	0	3	1	1	0	0	0	4	1	1	22	15	2
Lucas **Moura**	25	10	4	5	0	2	1	0	0	5	1	1	36	11	7
Tanguy **Ndombele**	12	9	2	1	1	0	0	0	0	4	2	0	17	12	2
Georges-Kevin **Nkoudou**	0	1	0	0	0	0	0	0	0	0	0	0	0	1	0
Troy **Parrott**	0	2	0	0	1	0	1	0	0	0	0	0	1	3	0
Danny **Rose**	10	2	0	0	0	0	0	0	0	4	0	0	14	2	0
Davinson **Sanchez**	27	2	0	3	1	0	1	0	0	5	0	0	36	4	0
Ryan **Sessegnon**	4	2	0	3	0	0	0	0	0	2	1	1	9	3	1
Moussa **Sissoko**	28	1	2	0	0	0	0	0	0	4	2	0	32	3	2
Oliver **Skipp**	1	6	0	1	0	0	1	0	0	0	2	0	3	8	0
Heung-Min **Son**	28	2	11	3	1	2	0	1	0	4	2	5	35	6	18
Japhet **Tanganga**	6	0	0	3	0	0	1	0	0	1	0	0	11	0	0
Jan **Vertonghen**	19	4	1	4	0	1	0	0	0	3	0	0	26	4	2
Michel **Vorm**	0	0	0	1	0	0	0	0	0	0	0	0	1	0	0
Malachi **Walcott**	0	0	0	0	0	0	0	0	0	0	1	0	0	1	0
Kyle **Walker-Peters**	3	0	0	0	0	0	1	0	0	1	0	0	5	0	0
Victor **Wanyama**	0	2	0	0	0	0	1	0	0	0	1	0	1	3	0
Harry **Winks**	26	5	0	5	0	0	0	0	0	5	0	0	36	5	0

INTRODUCING
PIERRE-EMILE
HØJBJERG

Our first major signing of the Summer 2020 transfer window was Danish international midfielder Pierre-Emile Højbjerg.

On 11 August 2020, we announced the signing of Pierre-Emile Højbjerg from fellow Premier League side Southampton. The Danish international midfielder arrived in N17 on the back of four impressive seasons with Saints, for whom he scored five goals in 128 appearances.

Højbjerg trained with the likes of BK Skjold, FC Copenhagen and Brøndby IF as a youngster and was named 'Danish U17 Player of the Year' in 2011 and 'Danish Talent of the Year' two years later. He moved to Bayern Munich in July 2012 and made his professional debut for the club against 1.FC Nürnberg in April 2013. Aged 17 years and 251 days at the time, he became the youngest player ever to represent Bayern in a Bundesliga match in the process.

The high-tempo midfielder started in Bayern's 2-0 extra-time DFB-Pokal Final victory over Borussia Dortmund in May 2014 during a campaign in which the Bavarians also won the Bundesliga title. He made his senior debut for Denmark against Sweden that same month. By the time of his transfer to Spurs in August 2020, Pierre-Emile had won a total of 33 caps for Denmark and scored three international goals.

Højbjerg spent loan spells with FC Augsburg and FC Schalke 04 during his time as a Bayern player. He departed the Allianz Arena to join Southampton on a five-year contract in July 2016, having made a total of 25 appearances for Bayern Munich. During his four seasons at St Mary's, he captained Southampton on a number of occasions and played in all five matches en route to the Saints' appearance in the 2017 EFL Cup Final at Wembley Stadium.

Just a week on from celebrating his 25th birthday on 5 August 2020, the Copenhagen-born player put pen-to-paper on a five-year contract with us. Speaking shortly after signing, Højbjerg – who wears our number five shirt – commented:

"From the first moment I got to speak to the people at the club, the coach, I think it was very clear to me that Spurs is a very big club but also a club with even more potential to reach the ultimate, and I wanted so much to be a part of that. I think there is a fantastic future ahead for the club and hopefully for me as well.

I think Spurs have fantastic players, a fantastic manager, a fantastic set-up and I feel lucky and proud to be a part of it. I want to give my everything but I also want to learn a lot. I want to be better and what was very important for me is that I wanted to play at a club where I could see myself for many years – and Tottenham was just the one. So, I'm very happy and proud to be here. The leaders and the players that we have… world class. And the coach also… world class. So again, to learn from them, to play with them and to see how they behave, it's a dream but it's also something that you have to learn from and get excited about – and I am, a lot!"

"I THINK SPURS HAVE FANTASTIC PLAYERS, A FANTASTIC MANAGER, A FANTASTIC SET-UP AND I FEEL LUCKY AND PROUD TO BE A PART OF IT"

WE ARE ONE

TOTTENHAM HOTSPUR

**2020/21
ONE HOTSPUR
MEMBERSHIP**
BRAND NEW
BENEFITS FOR
THIS SEASON

Find out more at
tottenhamhotspur.com/membership

WORDSEARCH

Can you find the names of EIGHT current and former Spurs players who have been the Club's top goal scorer during the Premier League era?

ADEBAYOR **BERBATOV** **KANE** **KLINSMANN**
BALE **DEFOE** **KEANE** **SHERINGHAM**

```
N  C  R  D  H  T  E  M  C  K
R  B  W  J  E  L  Z  Y  N  L
O  R  D  Q  A  F  J  T  L  I
Y  K  T  B  N  X  O  K  Q  N
A  Y  T  X  X  X  E  E  N  S
B  B  E  R  B  A  T  O  V  M
E  T  T  N  N  T  G  K  T  A
D  R  K  E  D  F  M  A  Y  N
A  R  N  D  W  Q  T  N  T  N
M  A  H  G  N  I  R  E  H  S
```

Answers on page 61

TOTTENHAM HOTSPUR

T.H
F.C.

AIA

TO DARE IS TO DO

WHEN THE YEAR ENDS IN
ONE

Throughout our 139-year history, we have experienced numerous trophy successes in years ending in one. As our players strive for glory in 2021, we look back on some of our past triumphs…

1901
FA CUP WINNERS

In 1901, whilst members of the old Southern League, we became the first and only non-league club ever to win the FA Cup. After drawing 2-2 with Sheffield United in the final at Crystal Palace, we beat the Blades 3-1 in the replay at Bolton's Burnden Park thanks to goals from John Cameron, Tom Smith and Sandy Brown.

1921
FA CUP WINNERS

Our second FA Cup triumph also came in a year ending in one, as we beat Wolverhampton Wanderers 1-0 in the final at Stamford Bridge, 100 years ago this season. Jimmy Dimmock scored the winner for Peter McWilliam's team, who finished sixth in the old First Division that same season.

1951
FOOTBALL LEAGUE CHAMPIONS

We became champions of England for the first time in 1951 as we finished four points clear of Manchester United to claim the First Division title. Our 'Push and Run' side, which was managed by former Spurs player, Arthur Rowe, won 25 of their 42 league matches that campaign, drew 10 and lost just seven, scoring 82 goals in the process.

1961
'DOUBLE' WINNERS

Bill Nicholson, who had been a key player in Rowe's title-winning side of 1950/51, guided us through our most successful season of all in 1960/61, as we became the first English club of the 20th century to win the Football League title and the FA Cup in a single campaign. More details of this glorious season can be found on pages 38 and 39 of this annual.

1971
FOOTBALL LEAGUE CUP WINNERS

Our inaugural season in the Football League Cup – currently known as the Carabao Cup for sponsorship reasons – came in 1966/67, while

Cyril Knowles and goalkeeper Pat Jennings proudly show off the League Cup trophy to fans on a lap of honour after the 1971 final.

we won the competition for the first time four seasons later. Martin Chivers scored twice in the 1971 League Cup Final as we beat Aston Villa 2-0 at the 'original' Wembley Stadium.

1981
FA CUP WINNERS

We returned to Wembley Stadium 10 years later to compete in the 100th FA Cup Final. Tommy Hutchison scored at both ends in our 1-1 draw with Manchester City. The replay saw Ricky Villa, who had been substituted in the game five days earlier, give us an eighth-minute lead. City equalised three minutes later through Steve MacKenzie and a penalty from Kevin Reeves early in the second half put them in front. Our striker Garth Crooks levelled with 20 minutes remaining prior to Villa scoring our winner – an effort that would go on to be voted Wembley Stadium's 'Goal of the (20th) Century' in 2001.

1991
FA CUP WINNERS

Our most recent FA Cup Final appearance got off to a somewhat inauspicious start as star midfielder Paul Gascoigne was stretchered off with a serious injury while Stuart Pearce gave opponents Nottingham Forest a 16th-minute lead with a thunderous free-kick. Our striker and current Match of the Day host Gary Lineker had a seemingly legitimate 'goal' ruled out for offside, while the England marksman also saw his 30th minute penalty saved by Forest goalkeeper Mark Crossley.

Paul Stewart equalised 10 minutes into the second half and in extratime, Des Walker scored an own goal to give us a 2-1 win. Having previously won the FA Cup in 1901, 1921, 1961, 1962, 1967, 1981 and 1982 we collected the trophy for a then-record eighth time.

2021 marks the 60th anniversary of the most successful season in our history – the 1960/61 campaign, which saw us win both the Football League championship and the FA Cup.

"We've got a good side here… we will win the double this season," was Danny Blanchflower's prediction before the start of the 1960/61 campaign. The Northern Irishman's claim was a particularly bold one given that prior to 1960, no club had managed to win the League and the FA Cup in a single campaign since Aston Villa way back in 1896/97.

QUICK START

Under the management of our former player Bill Nicholson, our class of 1960/61 made a remarkable opening to the campaign, winning 11 straight matches. No team in English top-flight history has since managed a better start to a season. The side remained unbeaten for the opening 16 games – dropping their first point in a

THOSE GLORY, GLORY DAYS

1-1 draw at Manchester City in October 1960. Our return to winning ways included triumphs over Nottingham Forest, Newcastle United, Cardiff City and Fulham before Sheffield Wednesday inflicted our first defeat of the season in mid-November.

Following home and away victories over West Ham either side of Christmas, we were 10 points clear of second-placed Wolverhampton Wanderers at the First Division summit by close of play on Boxing Day 1960, having won 21, drawn two and lost just one match.

In addition to our captain Blanchflower, other star players in our team that season included Scottish international goalkeeper Bill Brown and compatriots Dave Mackay and John White, Welsh wing wizard Cliff Jones and English forwards Bobby Smith and Les Allen. Bill Nick's regular starting XI during the campaign was completed by Peter Baker, Ron Henry, Maurice Norman and Terry Dyson.

DERBY DELIGHT

Our biggest home crowd of the season – 65,251 – saw us beat local rivals Arsenal 4-2 in the league in January 1961. Allen bagged a brace in that game while Smith – who ended up our top scorer that campaign with 33 goals – also netted, as did skipper Blanchflower from the penalty spot.

CUP RUN

Our road to FA Cup glory in 1960/61 began with a 3-2 triumph at home to Charlton Athletic. Allen, who scored 26 goals during the campaign, netted twice in the win while winger Dyson was also on target. Our FA Cup progress continued

DOUBLE DELIGHT

Goals from Smith and Dyson saw us triumph 2-0 against Leicester City in the FA Cup Final of 6 May, 1961. Over 100,000 fans were present at Wembley Stadium to witness Bill Nick's team become the first of the 20th century to complete the league and cup 'Double'.

ROLL CALL

Just 17 players featured for us during the 1960/61 season, with each individual's appearance information as follows…

with victories over Crewe Alexandra, Aston Villa, Sunderland and Burnley as we booked our place in the final.

CHAMPIONS

We went into our home match against title challengers Sheffield Wednesday on 17 April, 1961, knowing victory would be enough to see us crowned as First Division champions. A crowd of 61,205 packed into White Hart Lane to see the Monday evening match, which we led 2-1 at half-time thanks to strikes from Smith and Allen. With no further goals in the second half, the first part of the 'Double' had been achieved by Nicholson's men. The Football League Championship trophy was presented to skipper Blanchflower after the home game against West Bromwich Albion a few weeks later. We ended the season having won 31 of our 42 league fixtures while we drew four and lost seven matches scoring 115 goals in the process and conceding just 55. We amassed 66 points under the old two points for a win system – equivalent of 97 points today.

Player	App	Goals
Bill Brown (GK)	48	0
Peter Baker	48	1
Ron Henry	49	0
Danny Blanchflower	49	6
Maurice Norman	48	4
Dave Mackay	44	6
Cliff Jones	34	20
John White	49	13
Bobby Smith	43	33
Les Allen	49	26
Terry Dyson	47	17
Terry Medwin	16	6
Frank Saul	6	3
Tony Marchi	6	0
John Hollowbread (GK)	1	0
Ken Barton	1	0
John Smith	1	0

TOTTENHAM HOTSPUR STADIUM

Opened in 2019, Tottenham Hotspur Stadium is our multi-award-winning home ground…

Tottenham Hotspur Stadium officially opened its doors in April 2019 for our 2-0 Premier League victory over Crystal Palace and also staged the first leg of our UEFA Champions League semi-final against Ajax that same month.

Since its opening, accolades for the multi-purpose sports, leisure and entertainment

destination have been arriving thick and fast, including the Building Awards' 'Project of the Year', the Structural Awards' 'Supreme Award for Structural Engineering Excellence' and the AJ (Architects' Journal) Architecture Awards' 'Best Leisure Project'.

With a capacity of 62,303, Tottenham Hotspur Stadium is the largest club ground in London and the second largest in England. Designed by Populous, the venue has a host of unique features including the world's first dividing retractable pitch, enabling it to stage events such as NFL fixtures, rugby league and rugby union matches, boxing and concerts in addition to football.

Tottenham Hotspur Stadium – the first and only stadium outside of North America to be

STADIUM CAPACITY

62,303

specifically designed for NFL matches – hosted the NFL London Games in October 2019. The first fixture saw Oakland Raiders beat Chicago Bears 24-21 in front of a crowd of 60,463 while a similar number of fans saw the Tampa Bay Buccaneers take on the Carolina Panthers during the series.

The stadium is home to the largest single-tier stand in the country – the 17,500 capacity South Stand. Atop the South Stand roof is a scaled-up, fibreglass replica of the original Golden Cockerel, that once sat proudly on top of our former White Hart Lane home, which stands at almost 4.5m tall.

The four stands at Tottenham Hotspur Stadium are angled up to 35 degrees – the maximum permissible in British stadia design – which, combined with supporters' close proximity to the pitch, optimises atmosphere on matchday. The stadium is around 48m high, 250m long on its north–south axis and about 200m wide east to west, covering a total of 43,000m². Four large HD screens - the largest in the UK – are situated in the four corners of the stadium offering match action, replays and pre-match/half-time entertainment.

Outside the ground, the renovated Warmington House – originally built in 1828 – is home to the 'Tottenham Experience', which accommodates the Spurs Megastore – the largest football club shop in Europe – as well the forthcoming Club

Museum and Tottenham Hotspur Archive. Tottenham Hotspur Stadium was the subject of an episode of Richard Hammond's Big (Discovery Channel) in 2020, which saw the former Top Gear presenter visit our home ground and discover its advanced engineering and technological features. Hammond described the venue as "incredible" and "amazing" and added that "Tottenham Hotspur have created the ultimate, multi-purpose, high-tech, sporting stadium."

HEUNG-MIN SON
Scored the first-ever senior goal at Tottenham Hotspur Stadium

NICE ONE SON!

ONE ONE SON!

As he did in 2018/19, Heung-Min Son collected a clean sweep of end-of-season awards in 2019/20.

Heung-Min Son made it a 'double' quadruple as he was presented with the One Hotspur Player of the Season, One Hotspur Juniors' Player of the Season, Official Supporters' Clubs' Player of the Season and Goal of the Season awards after our final home match of the 2019/20 campaign against Leicester City. The South Korean international had previously won the same four awards at the end of 2018/19.

Today, is a bit disappointing because I play but you guys are not here [in Tottenham Hotspur Stadium due to COVID-19 restrictions]. Of course, it is a bit sad.

"This is a big honour for me, thank you so much. Thank you to my teammates also, thank you staff and thank you guys... amazing supporters during the season. It has been not a perfect season for us, but without you guys, we wouldn't achieve this position [of sixth in the Premier League table]."

> **Sonny netted 18 times in 41 appearances in all competitions during the 2019/20 season.**

Speaking to Spurs TV after the 3-0 victory over the Foxes in July 2020, Sonny commented;

"What should I say... thank you very much. It's a massive achievement for me. It was a bit different from last season (2018/19). Last season, I was suspended [for the final home game of the season] and I didn't play the game. One thing was good last season... the fans were fully here.

Sonny netted 18 times in 41 appearances in all competitions during the 2019/20 season. His amazing individual effort against Burnley on 7 December 2019 was, unsurprisingly, named both the BBC Match of the Day and the Premier League's 'Goal of the Month' for December 2019 and was subsequently named as BBC Match of the Day's 'Goal of the Season' too. Those fortunate enough to be able to witness the goal at Tottenham Hotspur Stadium will never forget the sight of our number 7 collecting the ball on the edge of his own penalty area before slotting the ball past the Clarets' goalkeeper Nick Pope just over 12 seconds later.

En route to scoring his 32nd-minute goal, the South Korean sprinted away from Robbie Brady and James Tarkowski with his initial burst, whilst also evading the attentions of Dwight McNeil. Having beaten Erik Pieters, he glided into the Burnley penalty area and beat Pope with a composed finish.

Recalling his effort after the game, Son said: "I saw Dele running on the left, and many players from Burnley. I tried to pass first of all to Dele; he was open but the right-back followed him and it was impossible to pass to him, so I just thought 'shall I go?' and put my booster on.

"It was the right timing to put the booster on! After two or three seconds I was in front of goal, really surprised and especially when you score this kind of goal at home it makes me so proud. It feels amazing.

"I was tired after the running! I was still focused on the finish and I wanted to finish it well. Imagine doing so well before the goal and missing - I'd have been really upset! I tried to focus and finish well. I'm really happy to score this goal."

Son has been no stranger to individual awards during his time at Spurs, which included him being named as the London Football Awards' Premier League Player of the Year in 2019. As

well as winning the same awards in 2018/19, he also collected the Goal of the Season accolade that campaign for his solo effort in our 3-1 win over Chelsea at Wembley on 24 November 2018. That strike was also voted as the Premier League's Goal of the Month for November 2018.

In December, 2019, meanwhile, Sonny was named AFC Asian International Player of the Year for a record third time, having previously collected the award in 2015 and 2017.

At the time of writing, he has been named the Korean Football Association Footballer of the Year on four occasions (2013, 2014, 2017 and 2019) and has claimed the Best Footballer in Asia crown five times (2014, 2015, 2017, 2018 and 2019).

Since signing for Spurs in August 2015, the South Korean has also twice been named as the Premier League Player of the Month, in September 2016 and April 2017.

43

TOP PREMIER LEAGUE 10 MATCHES

Editor Andy Greeves looks back at some of our most entertaining and significant league victories of the Premier League era.

10

Photo by: Shaun Botterill/Allsport

1995/96 Season
SPURS 4-1 MANCHESTER UNITED

With a number of key players including Darren Anderton, Ruel Fox and Gary Mabbutt all unavailable for our New Year's Day 1996 clash with Manchester United, few would have predicted a victory – let alone such a convincing one – against a team that went on to win the 'double' (the Premier League and FA Cup) that season. Our captain Teddy Sheringham's 35th-minute opener was cancelled out moments later by Andy Cole before Sol Campbell restored our lead just before the half-time break with a right-footed shot. Chris Armstrong's header put us 3-1 up just three minutes after the restart while the same player got to a Sheringham cross to round off our 4-1 win.

2007/08 Season
SPURS 6-4 READING

9

Dimitar Berbatov was our joint-top goal-scorer along with Robbie Keane in 2007/08 as he netted 23 times in all competitions during a highly productive campaign. One of the Bulgarian's major highlights that season was the four goals he scored in an incredible 6-4 victory over Reading at the Lane in December 2007. Berbatov's close-range effort gave us a seventh-minute lead in the match prior to Kalifa Cissé's leveller for the Royals. After Ívar Ingimarsson put Reading 2-1 up after eight minutes of the second-half, Berbatov levelled before the Berkshire side regained their advantage through a Dave Kitson strike. Our former number nine completed his hat-trick on 73 minutes while Kitson scored again seconds later. Steed Malbranque's goal made the score 4-4 with just 14 minutes of normal time remaining before a late strike from Jermain Defoe and Berbatov's fourth goal of the afternoon sealed our victory.

Background photo by: Michael Regan/Getty Images

Photo by: Hamish Blair/Getty Images

1999/2000 Season
SPURS 3-1 MANCHESTER UNITED

Manchester United arrived at White Hart Lane in October 1999 in a buoyant mood, having won the Premier League, the Champions League and the FA Cup the previous campaign. Sir Alex Ferguson's side led after 23 minutes of the encounter when Ryan Giggs collected a through-ball from Andy Cole and finished past Ian Walker. Our equaliser came on 37 minutes, when Steffen Iversen bundled home from close range. Three minutes later, Paul Scholes put through his own net from a David Ginola cross as we led 2-1 at the interval. Stephen Carr's 25-yard piledriver completed our impressive 3-1 victory with 19 minutes of the match remaining.

Photo by: Clive Brunskill / Allsport

Photo by: Alex Livesey/Getty Images

2015/2016 Season
MANCHESTER CITY 1-2 SPURS

Our 2-1 victory at Manchester City in February 2016 took us to within two points of Premier League leaders and that season's eventual title winners, Leicester City. Harry Kane put us in front from the penalty spot eight minutes into the second-half after Raheem Sterling was adjudged to have handled in his 18-yard-box. Substitute Kelechi Iheanacho looked to have gained City a point as he fired a Gael Clichy cross past Hugo Lloris. Christian Eriksen slotted home our winner, latching onto a magnificent through-ball from Erik Lamela with seven minutes of normal time left to play. We ended the campaign in third position in the Premier League table.

2006/07 Season
SPURS 2-1 CHELSEA

Prior to Chelsea's visit to White Hart Lane in November 2006, we hadn't beaten the Blues in a league match since February 1990. Claude Makelele collected a headed clearance from Ledley King and rifled the ball into the back of Paul Robinson's goal after 15 minutes of the game to give the visitors the lead. We levelled 10 minutes later, as Michael Dawson rose above the Chelsea backline to head home from a Jermaine Jenas free-kick. Aaron Lennon's memorable second-half winner saw him control an attempted clearance from Makelele, as he took the ball past Ashley Cole in the process before beating goalkeeper Henrique Hilario with his second touch.

Photo by: Mike Hewitt/Getty Images

5

Photo by: Laurence Griffiths/Getty Images

2016/17 Season
HULL CITY 1-7 SPURS

Our record away victory in the Premier League came on the final day of the 2016/17 Season. A brace from Harry Kane put us 2-0 up after just 13 minutes of our visit to the KCOM Stadium, while Dele Alli got our third goal of the day at the end of the first half. Hull pulled a goal back through Sam Clucas in the second period before Victor Wanyama restored our three-goal advantage on 69 minutes. Moments later, Kane completed his hat-trick while further strikes from Ben Davies and Toby Alderweireld rounded off our 7-1 win at the end of a campaign in which we finished as Premier League runners-up.

2009/10 Season
SPURS 2-1 ARSENAL

Classic matches against our local rivals Arsenal during the Premier League era include a 4-4 draw at the Emirates Stadium in October 2008 and a 2-1 win over the Gunners at White Hart Lane in February 2015 that saw Harry Kane score twice in his first senior north London derby. Another significant result against Arsenal came in April 2010. Danny Rose marked his Premier League debut in that match by scoring with a thunderous 30-yard volley past Manuel Almunia after just 10 minutes of the White Hart Lane match. Gareth Bale doubled our advantage a minute after half-time before Nicklas Bendtner got a late consolation for the visitors.

4

Photo by: Shaun Botterill/Getty Images

3

Photo by: Clive Rose/Getty Images

2009/10 Season
SPURS 9-1 WIGAN ATHLETIC

Our record victory of the Premier League era and our biggest-ever top-flight win came against Wigan Athletic in November 2009 in a match Jermain Defoe especially will never forget. Peter Crouch converted from an Aaron Lennon cross after just nine minutes, as we led 1-0 at the break. In the second half, Defoe proceeded to score one of the Premier League's fastest hat-tricks, with strikes on 51, 54 and 58 minutes, while Paul Scharner managed a goal back for Wigan in between. Lennon, who made numerous assists on the day, got on the scoresheet himself on 64 minutes before Defoe netted twice more. A late David Bentley free-kick and Niko Kranjcar's stoppage-time strike completed the rout.

2017/18 Season

CHELSEA 1-3 SPURS

Since the previously mentioned 2-1 win over Chelsea in November 2006, we have enjoyed a number of excellent home triumphs over the Blues, including a 5-3 victory on New Year's Day 2015. However, prior to our trip to SW6 in April 2018, we hadn't beaten Chelsea at Stamford Bridge in the Premier League era. After falling behind to an Alvaro Morata header, we equalised on the stroke of half-time, thanks to a wonder-strike from Christian Eriksen. Dele Alli put us in front just after the hour mark and his second strike of the afternoon just four minutes later sealed our first win at Stamford Bridge since February 1990.

2

1

2009/10 Season

MANCHESTER CITY 0-1 SPURS

Just a point separated ourselves and Manchester City in fourth and fifth place respectively in the Premier League table as we headed into the penultimate match of the 2009/10 season. Harry Redknapp's Spurs knew that a victory at the Etihad Stadium would guarantee a top-four finish and qualification to the UEFA Champions League play-off stage for the first time in our history. There were chances at either end on a tense night in M11, with Peter Crouch striking City's goal-frame at one stage. With eight minutes of the match remaining, Younes Kaboul went on a marauding run down the right side of the Citizens' penalty area. Goalkeeper Marton Fulop could only parry his cross and Crouch was on hand to head in the all-important winner.

EURO-VISION!

The COVID-19 pandemic brought about the postponement of the 16th European Championships until the summer of 2021. The tournament, which will still be known as UEFA Euro 2020, is set to get underway on 11 June 2021, as Italy host Turkey in Group A.

There is set to be plenty of Spurs involvement at UEFA Euro 2020, which will feature a total of 24 nations competing in 51 matches in 12 different cities across the continent. Wembley Stadium - our former, temporary home - has been earmarked to host three group stage matches, one round of 16 tie, both semi-finals and the showpiece final, which has been scheduled for 11 July 2021 at the time of writing.

Belgium were the first nation to book their place at the tournament back on 10 October 2019, with the 'Red Devils' later going on to win qualifying Group I. Past and present Spurs players such as Toby Alderweireld, Nacer Chadli, Mousa Dembele and Jan Vertonghen could be included in Roberto Martinez's squad for the tournament. Belgium are in Group B at Euro 2020 along with Denmark, Finland and Russia.

Ben Davies will be hoping to be involved for Wales, who line up in Group A at their second-successive tournament finals along with Italy, Switzerland and Turkey. Group C includes the Netherlands, for whom Steven Bergwijn made his senior debut in 2018. The 'Oranje' have 'home' advantage as they face group opponents including Ukraine and Austria in Amsterdam.

Speaking of 'home' advantage, much will be expected of Gareth Southgate's England side, who will play their Group D matches against the likes of Croatia and Czech Republic at Wembley Stadium. Harry Kane will be hoping to skipper the Three Lions at the tournament while Harry Winks, Eric Dier and Dele Alli have all been included in past Southgate squads.

Group E's line-up includes Spain, Sweden and Poland, while Portugal, who lifted the Henri Delaunay Trophy back in 2016, take their place in an ultra-competitive looking Group F, which features the likes of France and Germany. Hugo Lloris has won over 100 caps for Les Bleus and he could be joined in their squad by Moussa Sissoko and Tanguy Ndombele. Portuguese

international Gedson Fernandes, who signed for us on an 18-month loan in January 2020, could come up against a Club colleague or two when Portugal take on France.

Two teams from each group plus the four best-ranked third-placed teams at UEFA Euro 2020 qualify for the round of 16, with extra-time (two periods of 15 minutes each) and possibly, a penalty shoot-out, used to decide any knockout ties still level at the end of normal time.

FILL IN THE BLANKS

Fill in the various gaps in information on these two pages from league tables and matches involving Spurs as well as our Honours list.

LEAGUE TABLES

We won the First Division title in 1960/61. Can you complete our goal difference and points total from that season? (Remember, two points were awarded for a win and one point for a draw in the Football League until 1981/82 when the three points for a win system was introduced)

		P	W	D	L	GF	GA	GD	PTS
1	Spurs	42	31	4	7	115	55	+	
2	Sheffield Wednesday	42	23	12	7	78	47	31	58
3	Wolves	42	25	7	10	102	75	28	57
4	Burnley	42	22	7	13	102	77	25	51

Fill in our missing opponent from the UEFA Champions League Group B table in 2019/20

		P	W	D	L	GF	GA	GD	PTS
1		6	6	0	0	24	55	+19	18
2	Spurs	6	3	1	2	18	47	+4	10
3	Olympiacos	6	1	1	4	8	75	-6	4
4	Crvena zvezda	6	1	0	5	3	77	-17	3

Answers on page 61

HONOURS LIST

Fill in the gaps in our (chronologically-ordered) Honours List

Football League Winners

1950/51, 19____

Football League Cup Winners

19____, 1973,

19____, 20____

UEFA Cup Winners

1972, 1984

FA Cup Winners

1901, 19____, 1961, 1962, 1967, 1981, 19____, 19____

FA Charity/Community Shield Winners

1921, 1951, 19____, 1962, 1967*, 19____*, 1991*

*Shared

European Cup Winners' Cup Winners

1963

SCOREBOARD

Fill in the full-time scores from these memorable Spurs Premier League matches…

1995/96 Season

| Spurs | ☐ |
| Manchester United | ☐ |

2009/10 Season

| Spurs | ☐ |
| Wigan Athletic | ☐ |

2016/17 Season

| Hull City | ☐ |
| Spurs | ☐ |

2007/08 Season

| Spurs | ☐ |
| Reading | ☐ |

2009/10 Season

| Manchester City | ☐ |
| Spurs | ☐ |

2017/18 Season

| Chelsea | ☐ |
| Spurs | ☐ |

SCORERS

Fill in the missing goalscorers from selected Spurs Premier League victories in 2019/20…

Spurs 3 1 **Aston Villa**

Ndombele 73'   McGinn 9'
_____ 86', 90'

Spurs 5 0 **Burnley**

Kane 4', 54'
Lucas 9', Son 32'
_____ 74'

Spurs 4 0 **Crystal Palace**

_____ 10', 23'
Van Aanholt (OG) 21'
Lamela 42'

Spurs 2 0 **Brighton & Hove Albion**

Kane 53'   Webster 37'
_____ 72'

West Ham United 2 3 **Spurs**

Antonio 73'   Son 36'
Ogbonna 90+6'   _____ 43'
          Kane 49'

Spurs 2 0 **Manchester City**

_____ 63'
Son 71'

CROSSWORD

Answers
on page 61

ACROSS →

1 Type of bird represented on our Club crest. (8)
5 Our first Premier League opponents at the Tottenham Hotspur Stadium. (7,6)
7 The playing position of Hugo Lloris, Paulo Gazzaniga, etc. (10)
8 Our former home ground. (5,4,4)
9 Lucas Moura's nationality. (9)
11 Scored on his Premier League debut against Aston Villa in 2019 - Tanguy _____. (8)

DOWN ↓

1 One of our mascots. (6)
2 Trophy we have won on eight separate occasions. (2,3)
3 Abbreviation for Video Assistant Referee. (3)
4 Signed for us from Fulham in 2019 - Ryan _____. (9)
6 Surname of legendary former player and manager who led us to the 'Double' in 1960/61 - Bill _____.(9)
10 One of our mascots. (4)

SUPER SPURS QUIZ

1 From which Dutch club did we sign Steven Bergwijn in January 2020

2 What nationality is midfielder Giovani Lo Celso?

3 Who scored twice in our 3-2 victory over AFC Bournemouth at the Tottenham Hotspur Stadium in December 2019?

4 Which Spurs player captained France when they won the 2018 FIFA World Cup?

5 Against which Italian club did Harry Kane score a goal from the halfway line in the International Champions Cup in July 2019?

6 What role does Nuno Santos have at the Club?

7 Which teams competed in the first NFL fixture at the Tottenham Hotspur Stadium?

8 Who were our opponents in the 1961 FA Cup Final?

9 Who are the two Head Coaches of Spurs Women?

10 Which continental competition did Jose Mourinho win in 2004 whilst manager of FC Porto?

11 Who is our Assistant Head Coach?

12 Which former Top Gear host presented a 2020 television documentary exploring the Tottenham Hotspur Stadium?

13 In what round were we eliminated from the UEFA Champions League in 2019/20?

14 Who is our all-time, record goal-scorer?

ANSWERS ON PAGE 61!

KANE'S TOP 10 GOALS

With almost 200 strikes to choose from, Editor Andy Greeves selects 10 of Harry Kane's best goals in a Spurs shirt.

10 V BURNLEY (H)
Premier League
December 2019

In a match memorable for Heung-Min Son's incredible individual goal, Harry Kane scored with two wonderful efforts of his own in a 5-0 home win over Burnley in December 2019. His opening goal of the afternoon saw him collect a pass from Son before unleashing a powerful, right-footed shot from around 25 yards that Clarets goalkeeper Nick Pope had no chance of stopping.

9 V HUDDERSFIELD TOWN (A)
Premier League
September 2017

Kane's second goal in a 4-0 win at Huddersfield Town demonstrated a number of his qualities. Collecting a Kieran Trippier throw-in with his back to goal, the England skipper held the ball up before turning and moving into an area to curl a fine, left-footed shot past Jonas Lossl from the edge of the Terriers' 18-yard-box.

V EVERTON (H)
Premier League
March 2017

Continuing the theme of matches in which Harry has scored a memorable goal as part of a brace was his opener in a 3-2 triumph over Everton. Holding off a challenge from Idrissa Gueye midway inside the Toffees half, the striker moved forward and unleashed a thunderbolt from 25 yards that flew beyond the reach of Joel Robles at his near post.

V WOLVERHAMPTON WANDERERS (H)
Premier League
December 2018

Kane's opener against Wolves was one of our best goals of the 2018/19 season. The striker carried the ball to the edge of the visitors' penalty area before cutting inside with a Cruyff-esque turn and powering a shot into the far corner of Rui Patricio's net. Unfortunately, we lost 3-1 that day.

V ASTON VILLA (A)
Premier League
November 2014

Harry came on as a 58th-minute substitute for Emmanuel Adebayor as we trailed 1-0 in the Premier League match. After Nacer Chadli's equaliser, we were awarded a last-minute free-kick when Andros Townsend was felled by Villa defender Carlos Sanchez. Kane picked up the ball and hit a powerful shot which took a wicked deflection off Villa's Nathan Baker to give us a 2-1 win. The Walthamstow-born forward became a regular member of our starting XI for Premier League matches after this magical moment.

HARRY HAS A CANNY KNACK OF SCORING AGAINST ARSENAL!

5

V CHELSEA (H)
Premier League
January 2015

Kane scored twice in a memorable 5-3 victory over Chelsea on New Year's Day 2015 – both goals of which could be included in this 'Top Ten'. Of his two strikes, his first of the night, which cancelled out Diego Costa's opener, just edges it – an individual effort that saw him cut in from the left, evade the challenges of three Blues defenders before rifling a shot past Thibaut Courtois.

4

V ARSENAL (H)
Premier League
February 2015

Harry has a canny knack of scoring against Arsenal, with his penalty in the 2-2 draw at the Emirates Stadium in September 2019 seeing him become the fixture's joint-top goal scorer with 10 strikes, along with Bobby Smith and Emmanuel Adebayor. He netted twice in our 2-1 victory over the Gunners in February 2015 – his north London derby debut – which included a headed winner with only four minutes of regular time remaining.

3

V BORUSSIA DORTMUND (H)
UEFA Champions League
September 2017

In an interview, Kane named the first of his two goals in a 3-1 win over Borussia Dortmund in the UEFA Champions League in 2017 as one of his favourite European strikes for Spurs. Describing his effort against Dortmund, Harry said "I ran from the halfway line, got away from one player, got past another and scored from the angle." On the topic of the Champions League, an honourable mention must go to his cool finish against Barcelona at Wembley Stadium in 2018.

2

V JUVENTUS (N)
International Champions Cup
July 2019

Kane's match-winner in a pre-season tournament match against Juventus in 2019 brought inevitable comparisons with David Beckham's iconic, long-range goal for Manchester United against Wimbledon some 23 years earlier. In the third minute of added time at the end of the 90, Lucas Moura dispossessed Adrien Rabiot in the centre-circle. Kane moved towards the loose ball and struck it first time from just inside the Juventus half, lobbing former Arsenal goalkeeper Wojciech Szczesny from all of 50 yards.

NUMBER 1
V ARSENAL (H)
Premier League
March 2016

Having drawn level on the hour mark in our home match with Arsenal in March 2016, thanks to a Toby Alderweireld goal, Kane took the roof off White Hart Lane minutes later with an unforgettable strike. Collecting a flick from Dele Alli, our number '10' curled a magnificent shot past David Ospina from a tight angle on the edge of the Gunners' penalty area and promptly removed a protective face mask he was wearing for the game in celebration! The only disappointment was that we were unable to hold on for the win as the match finished in a 2-2 draw.

HUGO
LLORIS

TOTTENHAM
HOTSPUR

QUIZ/PUZZLE ANSWERS

PAGE 35 - WORDSEARCH

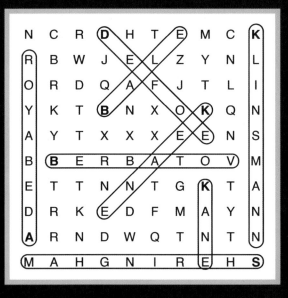

PAGE 52 - CROSSWORD

PAGE 54 - SUPER SPURS QUIZ

1) PSV Eindhoven
2) Argentinian
3) Dele Alli
4) Hugo Lloris
5) Juventus
6) Goalkeeper Coach
7) Oakland Raiders and Chicago Bears
8) Leicester City
9) Karen Hills and Juan Amoros
10) UEFA Champions League
11) Joao Sacramento
12) Richard Hammond
13) Round of 16
14) Jimmy Greaves

PAGE 50-51 – FILL IN THE BLANKS

League Tables

		P	W	D	L	G	GA	GD	PTS
1	Spurs	42	31	4	7	115	55	+ 60	66
2	Sheffield Wednesday	42	23	12	7	78	47	31	58
3	Wolves	42	25	7	10	102	75	28	57
4	Burnley	42	22	7	13	102	77	25	51

		P	W	D	L	GF	GA	GD	PTS
1	**Bayern Munich**	6	6	0	0	24	55	+19	18
2	Spurs	6	3	1	2	18	47	+4	10
3	Olympiacos	6	1	1	4	8	75	-6	4
4	Crvena zvezda	6	1	0	5	3	77	-17	3

Honours List

Football League Winners
1950/51, **1960/61**

FA Cup Winners
1901, **1921**, 1961, 1962, 1967, 1981, **1982**, 1991

Football League Cup Winners
1971, 1973, **1999**, **2008**

FA Charity/Community Shield Winners
1921, 1951, **1961**, 1962, 1967*, **1982***, 1991*
*Shared

Scoreboard

1995/96 Season	2009/10 Season	2016/17 Season
Spurs 4	Spurs 9	Hull City 1
Manchester United 1	Wigan Athletic 1	Spurs 7

2007/08 Season	2009/10 Season	2017/18 Season
Spurs 6	Manchester City 0	Chelsea 1
Reading 4	Spurs 1	Spurs 3

Scorers

Spurs 3	Ndombele 73', **KANE 86', 90'**
Aston Villa 1	McGinn 9'

Spurs 4	**SON 10', 23'**, Van Aanholt (OG) 21', Lamela 42'
Crystal Palace 0	

West Ham United 2	Antonio 73', Ogbonna 90+6'
Spurs 3	Son 36', **LUCAS 43'**, Kane 49'

Spurs 5	Kane 4', 54', Lucas 9', Son 32', **SISSOKO 74'**
Burnley 0	

Spurs 2	Kane 53', **DELE 72'**
Brighton 1	Webster 37'

Spurs 2	**BERGWIJN 63'**, Son 71'
Aston Villa 0	

CAN YOU FIND CHIRPY?